Long Term Care

It Doesn't Have To Be Expensive

A Guide For When Everything Feels Like Too Much

By: Ray Alkalai

Ray Alkalai

Long Term Care – It Doesn't Have To Be Expensive

This book and the insurance strategies in it aren't approved or endorsed by the Social Security Office or any other government agency.

Any guarantees depend on the financial strength and ability of the insurance company to pay claims.

This book is meant to give general information. Because of IRS rules, it is not legal or tax advice, and you can't use it to avoid penalties or promote or recommend any tax plan. Please talk with your own tax advisor or attorney for guidance.

All examples in this book are pretend situations meant to help you understand the ideas. They are not promises of results or performance.

Work with a Care Funding Specialist to build a strategy that works for you and your family.

Ray Alkalai

Long Term Care – It Doesn't Have To Be Expensive – A Guide For When Everything Feels Like Too Much

Copyright 2025 By H. Ray Alkalai

No part of this book may be copied or shared in any form, electronic or paper, without written permission from the publisher. The only exception is for reviewers, who may quote short sections in a review for a magazine, newspaper, or website.

The author and publisher worked hard to make sure the information in this book is accurate and complete, but we cannot guarantee there are no mistakes. We are not responsible for any errors or missing information. Any unintentional mentions of people, places, or organizations are purely accidental.

Our prime purpose in this life is to help others. And if you can't help them, at least don't hurt them.

Dalai Lama

Ray Alkalai

Long Term Care – It Doesn't Have To Be Expensive

Table of Contents

Acknowledgements 11

Lonae's Tragic End and the Silver Lining of It All… 13

Chapter 1: 19

The Hard Truth About Long-Term Care: Why Most Families Aren't Ready 19

Chapter 2: 23

How to Choose the Right Care, Before a Crisis Forces Your Hand 23

Chapter 3: 31

How to Get Paid, Get Support, and Get a Break While Caring for an Aging Parent 31

Chapter 4: 39

The Simple Home Changes That Help Seniors Stay Independent Longer 39

Chapter 5: 43

The Hidden Gap in Your Health Insurance Coverage, And How to Fix It 43

Chapter 6: 49

The Truth About Medicaid: What Families Don't Learn Until It's Too Late 49

Chapter 7: 57

The Complete Guide to Long Term Care Insurance, Without the Confusion 57

Chapter 8: 67

Turn Existing Annuities Into Tax Free Long-Term Care Benefits, Even With Health Issues 67

Chapter 9: 71

When Long-Term Care Is Needed Now: A Smart Strategy Many Families Overlook 71

Chapter 10: 75

The Smart Money Move... Protect Your Savings Without 'Use It or Lose It' Insurance 75

Chapter 11: 79

A Smarter Way to Use Your IRA: Care Benefits and Legacy in One Move 79

Chapter 12: 83

The Legal Documents Every Family Must Have Before Care Is Needed 83

Chapter 13: 89

Medicaid Myths vs. Reality: How Smart Planning Protects Your Life Savings 89

Chapter14: 93

Aid & Attendance: The Tax Free Income Most Veterans Never Hear About 93

Chapter 15: 99

Don't Go It Alone: How to Pick Advisors Who Actually Know Long-Term Care 99

Chapter 16: 107

Why "I'll Self-Insure" Is the Most Expensive Myth in Long-Term Care 107

Conclusion 111
Resources 113
Bonus Chapter: long-term care funding checklist & next steps
.... 115
About the Author 125
Summary 127

Ray Alkalai

Acknowledgements

To my wife Jackie... you carried the weight of our home on your shoulders, dealing with a sometimes–high-maintenance "employee" like me, and then somehow found room in your heart to be the daughter to my mom in all the ways I couldn't. The love, patience, and strength you showed her is something I'll never forget, and I don't think I could ever thank you enough for it. To my kids Alon and Andrea who had no idea I could either read or write, I appreciate you being more like me than I would like to admit.

To the entire Senior Care community here in the Twin Cities, there really aren't words big enough. Over the past few years, through both business and personal experiences, I've seen firsthand how rare you are. Nurses, administrators, home-care providers, caregivers, even the moving teams who help families through impossible transitions... you show up with compassion and grit every single day. You deserve far more recognition than you ever receive. You are extraordinary.

Ray Alkalai

Lonae's Tragic End and the Silver Lining of It All…

I never planned to write a book. What I wanted was something simple, a guide I could hand to families so they wouldn't have to go through what my mother and I went through. Something that would spell out the things we had to learn the hard way.

Because in my family, we lived both sides of the long-term care story. For one parent, there was no plan at all. For the other, the plan was there, waiting in the background, even though she never got the chance to use it.

It started in 2007. My parents were overseas on a long trip, just enjoying life. Eleven days in, I got a frantic phone call: my father was in a foreign hospital, feeling sick, and they weren't going to let him leave the country until someone figured out how to pay the bill.

I scrambled through calls, trying to find someone who could help, trying to get my parents home. Once they landed and the doctors ran the tests, we got the diagnosis no family ever wants to hear, lung cancer. That was April of 2007.

From that moment on, life shifted into survival mode.

My mother, Lonae, became everything. The driver. The caregiver. The cook. The nurse. The advocate. She carried the weight of every appointment, every medication, every impossible decision. She did it all alone because my wife and I were raising very young kids, working full-time, and we had no other family in town.

There weren't guides back then. There weren't checklists or YouTube channels or easy answers. My mother just pushed through the fog day after day, caring for my father as he endured chemo, radiation, endless medications, and a slow, painful decline. He lost half his body weight. She lost her strength and health trying to keep him alive.

He passed on December 26, 2007 at the age of 70, six months after the oncologist told me that it was all the time we had left with him.

Life moved on, but the weight of those months never really left us.

In 2019, when my mom was 78, I sat down with her to go over her finances. Parents never enjoy talking about money with their kids, but this was long overdue.

That's when I found the $100,000 CD earning 0.17%. This was 2018ish.

I asked her what it was for. She said, "Just in case I need nursing home care."

And here's what hit me: after all the years I'd been in this profession… after everything we lived through with my father… she still didn't really understand what I did or how planning could protect her.

So we talked. And I showed her what was possible.

We took that $100,000 and purchased an asset-based long-term care policy — the kind you'll learn about later in this book. It turned her $100,000 into $260,000 of long-term care benefits, more than $4,100 per month for five years if she ever needed help.

She never got a chance to use it.

Because of how asset-based LTC works, that meant something powerful: when she passed, my sister and I received the money back. The plan still protected her, just in a different way. **It was her peace of mind.**

It all started in 2023, everything began to change. The woman who once walked through foreign cities for days without slowing down suddenly struggled to walk across her living room. Her back pain grew worse through December 2024. Doctors couldn't find the cause. A spine surgeon eventually recommended surgery as a "Hail Mary."

We took it.

She had her first surgery end of February of 2025. It didn't help her mobility. Over the next few months her body weakened. Her right leg, then her right arm. More specialists. More consultations. More pain. Then a second surgery.

Around six months after that first surgery, she was gone.

In between, it was a battle. I put cameras in her house just to keep her safe. When the alert went off the day she fell, her sixth fall, I rushed over. She was wedged between the bed and the wall, unable to move. I called 911.

After the hospital came the Transitional Care Unit, a TCU. A place meant to help people get stronger so they can go home. The intent is good. The experience... is something else.

You improve a little, then stall, then decline. The staff try, but the system works against them. Medicare paid for 78 of the 100 days she qualified for, but it wasn't automatic. I fought every step of the way through 5 appeals. Every week approximately Medicare Advantage wanted to kick her out of the TCU. I learned how to appeal, how to challenge the rules, how to push back against a system that seems designed to wear families out until they stop fighting.

Eventually, despite everything, she developed a bowel obstruction from the medications and went back to the hospital. That was the end of her journey.

I'm sharing this because I want you to see the truth: we can't control when life falls apart.

But we can control whether we're prepared **before** it does.

And preparation doesn't erase the pain, but it absolutely changes the experience. In our case, my mother had resources. She had savings. She had that asset-based plan that would have covered much of her care if she needed it. Because she didn't use it, it still returned value to her kids. We weren't drowning. We weren't choosing between paying bills or paying for help. We weren't financially crushed while emotionally exhausted.

Many families don't get that luxury.

The number one question that destroys families is, **"How are we going to pay for this?"** And when you're asking that question in the middle of a crisis, you're already losing ground.

That's why I wrote this book. Not to scare you. Not to guilt you, But to show you the path forward.

You don't have to cover everything. You just need to cover enough. Enough to protect your family. Enough to avoid being a burden. Enough to make sure the people you love don't have to fight the system while fighting to keep you safe.

If my story becomes the moment you finally decide to plan… then everything my mother lived through, everything we endured together, will help someone else avoid the same pain.

That's my hope. That's why this book exists. And that's why I'm inviting you to turn the page and start planning now, while you still can.

Ray Alkalai

Chapter 1:

The Hard Truth About Long-Term Care: Why Most Families Aren't Ready

The Money Question Everyone Faces

When seniors think about long-term care, the first question is almost always the same: *How are we going to pay for this?*

According to the 2024 www.CareScout.com cost of care website, the numbers look like this:

- A private nursing-home room averaged **$350 per day**; a semi-private room averaged **$305 per day**.
- Assisted living cost an average of **$5,900 per month**.
- Home health aides averaged **$34 per hour**, homemaker services averaged **$33 per hour**, and adult day services averaged **$100 per day**.

Privately paying for long-term care means a family could need an extra **$60,000 to $130,000 per year** for just *one* person. Most people—at any age—can't absorb that kind of ongoing expense.

Why Insurance Matters

Long-term care insurance covers in-home support, assisted living, and nursing-home care. It protects your lifestyle, not just where you receive care. If you picture yourself staying in your own home, in your own chair, with your own TV and routines, this type of insurance helps make that possible.

Today's policies include several updated options, including new guaranteed-issue choices that appeared after the COVID-19 pandemic. Later chapters walk through these in detail.

Using Home Equity as a Tool

Reverse mortgages (Home Equity Conversion Mortgages) have become a common way to pay for care. They help seniors stay at home longer by covering costs like in-home support, repairs, and accessibility updates. This strategy shows up throughout this book because it has become a key part of cash-flow planning for many older adults.

Government Programs That Can Help

Medicaid will pay for long-term care, but eligibility is strict. Before applying, seniors should speak with both a care funding professional and an elder-law attorney.

Veterans Directed Care allows eligible Veterans to choose who provides their care. **VA Aid and Attendance** offers additional pension benefits for qualifying Veterans and spouses who served during a period of war.

Both programs are covered in more detail later.

Who Will Care for Mom and Dad?

A joint Cornell–Purdue study found aging mothers are almost **four times** more likely to expect a daughter, not a son, to provide care if they become ill. And according to AARP, **1 in 5 Americans**, or more than **53 million people**, provide unpaid family care.

Parents often choose the child they feel closest to and who shares similar values. While older adults today may have had larger families, that doesn't make these conversations any easier. Families who avoid talking about expectations often face confusion, resentment, or conflict later.

Long-term care is a family issue, but it is overwhelmingly a women's issue. Women traditionally carry the caregiving load, and they also tend to live longer than men. Many serve in what's called the **"sandwich generation,"** caring for aging parents while still raising children. Careers get delayed, promotions missed, and finances strained.

Since COVID-19, more caregivers are using Medicaid's Consumer Directed Care program, which allows certain family members to be paid for providing care.

Women also typically marry older men, meaning many become the primary caregiver for a spouse later in life. When family assets are spent on the ill spouse, the surviving spouse can be left with little support.

Statistically, **1 in 2 women** and **1 in 3 men** will need long-term care during their lifetime. Women's longer life expectancy explains the difference.

How Long Can Seniors Realistically Stay at Home?

Staying at home depends on many factors: support from family or neighbors, access to healthcare, and available cash flow.

A National Association of Home Builders 50+ Housing Council study found that **35.9%** of adults aged 55–64 living in single-family homes reported at least one difficulty with daily activities:

- dressing **(9%)**
- vision or hearing **(11%)**
- going out **(11.9%)**
- walking, lifting, climbing stairs, or getting around the home **(27.1%)**
- remembering **(12.7%)**
- working **(23.8%)**

Among adults 65–74, more than **45%** reported difficulty. For those 75 and older, the number rose to **70%**.

The truth is simple: seniors *can* stay safely in their homes for life if care is properly arranged, the living space is safe, and funding is available. The next chapters explain practical ways to make that happen.

Chapter 2:

How to Choose the Right Care, Before a Crisis Forces Your Hand

Many families want to keep their aging loved ones at home as long as possible. If that's your goal, choosing the right home care agency is a major step. Here are the key things to look for.

Practical Tips for Selecting a Home Care Agency

- Stay organized and clear about what you need.
- Ask if the agency has a backup caregiver when someone is sick or doesn't show.
- Give the caregiver a daily checklist of tasks.
- Caregivers should not sleep or smoke in your home.
- Call the agency right away if the caregiver isn't meeting expectations.
- Caregivers bring their own meals unless you offer otherwise.
- Don't tip.
- Don't allow your loved one to ride in the caregiver's car unless the agency approves it in advance.

- Caregivers should keep personal phone use to a minimum.
- Understand how and when payment is expected.
- Some aides are Certified Nurse's Aides (CNAs) and some are not. CNAs may take blood pressure and pulse, while others may not. Ask the agency about training.
- In the first week or two, schedules may shift. Once things settle, you should see the same caregiver consistently.
- Ask about the agency's hiring and screening process. Do they run background checks and check abuse registries? Are they bonded and insured?
- If there are repeated late arrivals, no shows, or poor service, speak up. If it doesn't improve, it may be time to switch agencies.

Medical vs. Non-Medical Home Care

Home care comes in two main forms: **nonmedical** and **medical**.

Non-Medical Home Care

These caregivers help with:

- light housekeeping, laundry, errands, and groceries
- prescription pickups
- simple meal preparation
- social activities like watching TV, playing games, going to events, or visiting the library
- transportation (only if approved in advance)
- bathing, dressing, medication reminders, and help moving from bed to chair

Medical Home Care

These services include:

- physical, occupational, or speech therapy
- wound care
- skilled nursing tasks

No agency will care for your parent exactly the way you would, but a good one will send people who are compassionate and dependable. Do your homework, check in often, drop by unexpectedly, and communicate clearly with the agency.

Also, recognize that when you work with one agency compared to another, we are human. Sometimes it's an issue of personalities that do not connect and it is OK to change. Its about your comfort not the agencies. Be an advocate for yourself and speak up.

Choosing an Adult Day Services Center

Adult day centers are a growing alternative to nursing homes. They give seniors a safe and social place to spend the day while allowing them to continue living at home. Most centers provide meals, activities, medication administration, and sometimes transportation. Some accept Medicaid, but many prefer private pay or long-term care insurance.

Tips for Finding a Good Adult Day Center

- Start by identifying centers in your area through:
    - online searches
    - your local Area Agency on Aging (AAA) at **1-800-677-1116**
    - senior centers
    - your doctor
    - a geriatric care manager
- Call centers and ask for:
    - brochures or flyers
    - eligibility requirements
    - monthly activity calendars
    - menus
    - application details

What to Look For

- Who owns or runs the center
- How long it has operated
- Openings and waitlists
- Licensing or certification (if required)
- Hours and days of operation
- Transportation options
- Costs and any additional fees
- Medical conditions accepted (memory loss, limited mobility, incontinence)
- Staff training and staffing ratios
- Variety of activities
- Menu options

After reviewing materials, schedule tours at two or more centers. Check references from families who have used the center. Try the center for three to five days, adjusting takes time. If issues come up, ask for a meeting to make the transition smoother.

Choosing an Assisted-Living Facility

Assisted living offers a middle ground between independent living and nursing homes. Residents usually have their own apartment (often without a kitchen) and receive:

- three meals a day
- help with medications
- laundry, housekeeping, and linen service
- assistance with bathing or dressing if needed
- social activities and transportation

Costs range from **$2,800 to $12,000 per month**, depending on location. These can be paid with private funds or long-term care insurance. Facilities may stand alone or be part of a larger retirement community.

I will sometimes refer to these facilities as a stationary cruise ship. Just like in the cruise ship industry, there are 2 star and 5 star services. They all mean well, its up to you to figure out what works for you.

Nursing Home Care

When assisted living is no longer enough, nursing homes provide 24-hour care from trained staff. A Registered Nurse (RN) or Licensed Practical Nurse (LPN) is always on duty.

Nursing homes vary:

- Some are private pay only.

- Some accept Medicare for a limited time.
- Others accept Medicaid.

Most residents live in semi-private rooms, though private rooms are an option if you can afford them. There are programs that allow you to bring plants, animals, and children into the environment to create a more home-like feel. Ask about what programs are available in the facility.

In 2024, the national average cost for a semi-private room was **$305 per day** or **$9,150 per month.**

Tips for Choosing an Assisted-Living or Nursing-Care Facility

Choosing a facility takes time and patience. Be prepared, especially for specialized memory-care units, which often have waitlists, due to a quickly aging population and living longer, of **6 to 18 months.**

Key tips:

- Talk to people you trust about their experiences.
- Location matters, choose one that's easy to visit.
- Ask about bed availability and whether they accept Medicare, Medicaid, or private pay.
- Learn about staffing levels (RNs, LPNs, CNAs).
- Ask about extra services and fees.
- Make sure they can handle specific medical needs like Alzheimer's or End-Stage Renal Disease.
- Tour every facility you're considering.
- Review their latest state inspection or visit **medicare.gov** for ratings.

Long Term Care – It Doesn't Have To Be Expensive

- Notice how residents seem to be living, do they look comfortable and cared for?
- Ask how long staff members have worked there.
- Confirm background checks are performed.
- Pay attention to sights and smells when you walk in.
- Review visiting hours and safety procedures, including fire plans.
- Visit at least once unannounced.
- Make an inventory of everything your loved one brings and label all items.
- Speak with other families visiting the facility to hear their experiences.
- If possible opt for a couple of weeks of respite care to try it out
- **Trust me on this: Put cameras in the room.**

Ray Alkalai

Chapter 3:

How to Get Paid, Get Support, and Get a Break While Caring for an Aging Parent

Where Can They Turn When They Need A Break?

One out of every four U.S. families is caring for an aging adult. For some, this means round-the-clock support. For others, it means driving a parent to appointments or helping with errands. Over the last decade, elder care has replaced childcare as the biggest challenge for working adults, and employers feel the impact too.

Caring for a parent can be meaningful, but it can also be exhausting. When the roles reverse, the emotional weight is real.

When helping my mother in her last 8 months of life I calculated approximately 14-20 hours a week were spent on just her needs. From setting appointments, and getting her there, to dealing with any facility or service issue she was having in addition to just visiting her. It feels exhausting.

Respite Care: Why Caregivers Need Time Off

Respite care gives caregivers a break, time to rest, reset, and handle personal tasks. Without it, stress builds and the quality of care can decline. There are several ways families can get respite support.

In-Home Respite

You can arrange in-home care for a few hours or several days. Key points:

- Choose an agency with a strong reputation.
- Confirm background and abuse checks for all caregivers.
- Long stretches of care can be expensive, so budget ahead.
- Many agencies require advance notice for multi-day coverage.

Respite in a Facility

Assisted living communities and nursing-care facilities often offer short-term stays.

- Stays may require a minimum number of days.
- Costs include room and board; extras may cost more.
- Some facilities allow short notice, others need several weeks.
- Check local availability early.

Volunteer-Based Programs

Local Area Agencies on Aging or social service groups sometimes send volunteers for short visits.

- Volunteers are not medical professionals.
- Best for providing short breaks and light companionship.
- Usually low cost or free for residents.

Alzheimer's Association Resources

Your local Alzheimer's Association can provide referrals, even if your loved one does not have Alzheimer's. They often have extensive databases of support programs.

Leaning on Family and Friends

Don't hesitate to ask for help.

- Hold a brief family meeting.
- Ask each person to contribute 1–2 hours a week.
- Create a schedule so everyone knows their role.

Faith and Community Groups

Churches and community organizations often send volunteers for short visits. Like volunteer programs, these helpers are not medical caregivers but can offer relief.

Taking care of yourself matters. If you burn out or become ill, your loved one loses their main support. Ask for help. It may be more available than you think.

Hospice Care at the End of Life

Hospice is NOT a bad word. If you know its end of life type situation, than get as much info as possible about hospice options. Hospice can make your life and your loved ones life better so Learn about it early.

Hospice supports people who are expected, by a physician, to have six months or less to live. The focus is comfort, managing pain, offering emotional support, and helping the family.

Hospice can take place:

- at home
- in a hospice facility
- in a long-term care facility

Coverage is available through **Medicare, Medicaid, most private insurance, and long-term care insurance**.

Hospice uses a team approach that may include:

- physicians
- nurses
- home health aides
- clergy or social workers
- trained volunteers
- physical or occupational therapists

Medical supplies, equipment, and licensed nursing care are covered by Medicare or private insuranceHowever, families must pay privately—or use long-term care insurance—when they need 24-hour home health aides or unlicensed support. Most long-term care policies cover hospice immediately, without requiring an elimination period.

Paying Yourself or a Loved One for Providing Care

Options and Tax Advantages

Many adult children cannot afford to quit their jobs to provide full time care. There are legal and financial tools that can help.

Caregiver Contracts

Seniors can pay family members for care using a formal caregiver contract drafted by an elder law attorney. This treats the arrangement like hiring a care agency.

Long-Term Care Insurance

Some long-term care insurance policies reimburse family caregivers for providing approved care.

Guaranteed-Issue Long-Term Care Annuities

These annuities, which follow Pension Protection Act rules, allow tax-free withdrawals to pay friends or family members for care at home.

Underwritten Immediate Annuities

New immediate annuities designed for people already receiving care may offer higher income once the person cannot perform **2 of the 6 activities of daily living** or has cognitive decline. More information on this later in the book.

Medicaid Consumer Directed Care

Individuals on Medicaid may choose a family member to provide their care at home and receive payment through Medicaid.

Veterans Directed Care

Veterans who qualify can choose a friend or family member to provide care, paid for through the VA.

Tax Deductions and Benefits for Caregivers

To claim an aging parent as a dependent, all of the following must be true:

1. You provide more than half of their financial support.
2. They are a relative or a non-relative who lived with you all year or are in assisted living or a nursing home.
3. They are a citizen of the U.S., Canada, or Mexico.
4. They do not file a joint tax return that year.

Qualifying deductible expenses include:

- medications
- long-term care insurance premiums
- home modifications
- transportation to medical appointments
- private in-home care
- wheelchairs, eyeglasses, dentures
- any cost tied to long-term care needs not covered by insurance
- a percentage of assisted-living expenses
- **all** costs of nursing-home care if paid privately

Long Term Care – It Doesn't Have To Be Expensive

Because these rules get complex, consulting a tax advisor or elder-law attorney is essential, especially when multiple siblings share costs, Medicaid may be needed, or a caregiver contract is involved.

Child and Dependent Care Credit

If you hired someone to care for your loved one so you could work, you may qualify for the **Child and Dependent Care Credit**, worth up to **35%** of eligible expenses depending on income.

To claim the credit:

- You must have earned income.
- You cannot pay someone you claim as a dependent or your child under age 19.
- You must file as single, head of household, qualified widow(er) with a dependent child, or married filing jointly.
- Care must be provided by a qualifying individual.
- The dependent must live with you more than half the year.

Local tax advisors can help you explore related state level deductions.

Using a Dependent Care FSA

A **Dependent Care FSA** lets employees set aside pre-tax dollars to pay for elder-care expenses, including certain medical and day-care costs. Important details:

- Funds must be used by the end of the plan year or grace period.
- If an elderly parent lives with you and depends on you for at least 50% of their support, the FSA can be used for day-care expenses.
- Care must be necessary for you (and your spouse, if married) to work, look for work, or be a full-time student.
- FSA dollars cannot be used for custodial nursing care.

Proper planning ensures you don't contribute more than you can use.

Chapter 4:

The Simple Home Changes That Help Seniors Stay Independent Longer

Keeping seniors safe at home starts with making sure their space is easy to navigate, updated, and accessible. Both the inside and outside of the home play a major role in preventing accidents and supporting independence.

Making the Home Senior-Friendly

Interior Safety

Simple changes can dramatically reduce risk:

- Install grab bars in the bathroom.
- Use elevated toilet seats and lower vanities or sinks if needed.
- Lower kitchen cabinets for easier access.
- Widen narrow doorways in older homes for walkers and wheelchairs.
- Replace round doorknobs with lever handles.
- Remove throw rugs, they are one of the most common causes of falls.

Exterior Safety

Outside the home:

- Add sturdy handrails near steps and uneven pavement.
- Consider no-step entryways at the front door or garage.

Many contractors now specialize in senior-friendly home design. For a more complete list of modifications, visit www.AgingInPlace.com.

Personal Emergency Response Systems (PERS)

A Personal Emergency Response System is one of the most effective tools for helping seniors stay safe and independent.

These systems are affordable and easy to install. A senior wears a small pendant or watch device and can call for help at the push of a button, whether they fall, get sick, or feel unsafe.

This isn't just for those already struggling with health issues. PERS helps *healthy* seniors stay well by giving them immediate support when something goes wrong.

What the Statistics Show

- Seniors with a PERS stay at home **6 years longer** on average than those without one (AC Nielsen).

- Many systems include smoke-detector options for added safety.
- **58%** of users with a PERS for at least a year say their quality of life improved.
- **87%** feel the protection is important to staying at home.
- **95%** feel safer at home.
- **80%** value the comfort of living in their own home.
- **76%** say independence is important to them.
- Seniors with a PERS reported greater ability to carry out daily routines and were **ten times less likely** to need nursing-home admission.
- Nearly **1 in 3 adults over 65**, and **half of adults over 90**, fall each year.
- **30%–50%** of elderly adults fear falling, often limiting activities and confidence. PERS helps reduce this fear and the isolation that comes with it.

Why PERS Makes a Difference

- Recommended by doctors, nurses, and caregivers because quick help prevents long-term harm.
- Helps seniors live independently at home instead of moving into assisted living, nursing homes, or needing 24-hour care.
- Useful even when seniors don't live alone, accidents can happen when the other person steps out.
- The help button is small, simple, and doesn't interfere with daily activities.
- Some PERS phones offer extra features like easier calling and personalized reminders.

Ray Alkalai

Chapter 5:

The Hidden Gap in Your Health Insurance Coverage, And How to Fix It

Does Medicare Pay for Long-Term Care?

There is **a common misunderstanding** about health insurance and long-term care. Many people assume Medicare or private insurance will pay for extended care needs, but they won't. These programs were never designed to cover long-term, custodial care.

What Medicare Actually Is

Medicare is a federal health insurance program for:

- people 65 and older
- certain people with disabilities
- those with End Stage Renal Disease (ESRD)

Medicare helps with many medical costs but not all of them. You are responsible for certain deductibles, co-pays, and gaps.

This is why many people buy Medicare Supplement plans or long-term care insurance.

Medicare was created in **1965** and has **never** been fully overhauled. Back then, life expectancy was lower and medical technology was limited. The system was built for **short-term** medical care, not chronic conditions like Alzheimer's, Parkinson's, or multiple sclerosis.

Even with the addition of Medicare Part D in 2004/2005, Medicare still does **not** pay for long-term care.

What Medicare Pays For

Medicare consists of four parts: A, B, C, and D.

Medicare Part A - Hospital Insurance

Covers:

- inpatient hospital care
- some skilled nursing facility care
- hospice care
- limited home health care (with qualifications)

Most people receive Part A automatically at age 65 with no premium.

Medicare Part B - Medical Insurance

Covers:

- doctor visits
- outpatient care
- medical services not covered under Part A

Part B has a monthly premium. In **2025**, the standard premium is **$185**, though it increases with higher income.

What Medicare Does NOT Pay For

Medicare's deductibles and limits create major out-of-pocket costs.

Hospital Deductibles (2025)

- Days 1–60: you pay **$1,676** total deductible
- Days 61–90: you pay **$419 per day**
- Days 91– and on: you pay **$838 per day**

Skilled Nursing Facility

- Days 1–20: Medicare pays 100%
- Days 21–100: you pay **$209.5 per day**
- After day 101: you pay **all costs**

Other Out-of-Pocket Costs

- **20%** of most Part B covered services
- **50%** of outpatient mental health treatment
- Co-pays for outpatient hospital care

I believe, as I hope you do as well, that costs are only going to go up and planning can mitigate for these additional expenses.

Skilled Care vs. Custodial Care

Skilled Care

Medically necessary care ordered by a doctor and performed by licensed professionals:

- wound care
- IV antibiotics
- physical therapy after a stroke

Medicare covers skilled care because it is short-term and rehabilitative.

Custodial Care

Daily assistance with:

- bathing
- dressing
- toileting
- transferring

Custodial care is **not** covered by Medicare and must be paid privately (out of your pocket) or through long-term care insurance.

Medicare Supplements (Medigap)

Medicare Supplement plans:

- cover deductibles and co-pays from Medicare Parts A and B
- are sold by private insurance companies
- do **not** pay for long-term custodial care

In **2025**, there were **10 standardized Medigap plans**. Each plan covers different gaps, but none cover long-term care expenses.

Medicare Advantage Plans (Part C)

Medicare Advantage plans combine:

- Part A
- Part B
- usually Part D

These plans operate like managed care networks (HMOs or PPOs). You may be restricted to certain doctors or facilities. Advantage plans may also limit hospital or rehab days. In addition the treatment of how long you get coverage if you need a transitional care unit after an event is much different than with a supplement.

Private Insurance and Disability Insurance

Private Health Insurance

Employer-sponsored or retiree health insurance works much like Medicare Advantage. No matter how good the benefits are, private health insurance does **not** cover ongoing long-term care.

Disability Insurance

Disability insurance replaces income and pays household expenses, rent, groceries, utilities. It is **not** intended to cover long-term care costs.

Long-Term Care Insurance

Long-term care insurance does what Medicare and health insurance do not. It pays for:

- in-home care
- assisted living
- nursing-home care
- adult day care

It also covers **custodial care**, which is the majority of long-term care needs.

Medicare Income-Related Premiums (2023)

Go to the link below to see the affects your monthly Medicare Part B premium increases base on income. Since the income ranges and costs change annually it is better if you see what it currently is using the link and a great Medicare Agent can help you understand the fine details.

Source: https://www.medicare.gov/Pubs/pdf/11579-medicare-costs.pdf

The Bottom Line

Medicare was **never** meant to pay for long-term care. If you need ongoing support, whether in a nursing home, assisted living, or at home, Medicare will not cover it.

That responsibility falls on long-term care insurance, personal savings, or family support.

Chapter 6:

The Truth About Medicaid: What Families Don't Learn Until It's Too Late

Medicaid was created under Title XIX of the Social Security Act and is run separately by each state. It serves people who are poor, medically needy, or facing high healthcare costs. Medicaid is meant to be a safety net for those who have no other way to pay for care, especially long-term care.

It is the **payer of last resort** for older adults with serious health issues, people with disabilities, and those needing ongoing support. States decide which optional services, like prescription drugs, dental care, and eyeglasses, they will cover. **When state budgets tighten**, these optional services are often **the first to be cut**.

Medicaid is also heavily strained. It is underfunded, overburdened, and subject to frequent state-level changes. These decisions affect eligibility rules, the number of people who qualify, and which services are paid for.

The Deficit Reduction Act of 2005

In 2006, the Deficit Reduction Act (DRA) tightened Medicaid's long-term care eligibility rules and expanded the Long-Term Care Partnership program.

The goal was to encourage people to plan ahead and buy private long-term care insurance, reducing pressure on Medicaid. States can now offer **Qualified State Long-Term Care Insurance (QSLTCI)** policies through the partnership model.

Key Changes to Medicaid Eligibility

The DRA made qualifying for Medicaid harder. Major changes include:

- A **5-year look-back period** for asset transfers.
- Applicants must meet spend-down requirements **before** their penalty period begins.
- Medicaid coverage is denied for anyone with home equity above **$788,000** in Minnesota as of this writing and there are exceptions. These limits are indexed for inflation. Every state has a different value.

Expansion of Partnership Long-Term Care Policies

Under the expanded Partnership program, states can offer long-term care policies that protect assets. These policies must meet federal guidelines and match the benefits of non-partnership policies.

Partnership policies allow consumers to protect assets **dollar for dollar** equal to the benefits paid by the policy. This helps people avoid spending down all their savings before qualifying for Medicaid.

Assets You Must Spend Down Before Medicaid

Countable assets include:

- cash, checking, and savings
- CDs, savings bonds
- investment accounts
- IRAs and retirement accounts
- vacation homes or investment property
- a second car
- personal property not in use

Assets You Can Keep

Non-countable assets include:

- your home (within your state's equity limit)
- household goods and personal items
- one vehicle
- life insurance with up to **$1,500** in cash value currently in Minnesota
- irrevocable prepaid burial plans
- property essential for self-support
- income-producing property (with limits)

Reverse Mortgages and Medicaid

Reverse mortgages do **not** affect Medicare or Social Security, but they can affect Medicaid and local income-based programs.

Before taking a reverse mortgage, seniors should consider key questions:

- Are they in poor health?
- Do they plan to gift money to family?
- Will they use the money for in-home care?
- Do they already have long-term care insurance?
- Do they expect to apply for Medicaid soon?

If any answer is "yes," they should consult an elder law attorney—ideally one familiar with both Medicaid and reverse mortgages.

Why This Matters

- Cash from a reverse mortgage can cause someone to lose Medicaid eligibility if not handled properly.
- Lump-sum withdrawals can create excess assets in checking or savings accounts.
- Money withdrawn from a line of credit must be **spent in the same month** and documented with receipts.
- Monthly payouts increase income and may push someone over Medicaid's income limits.

In short: if Medicaid is needed soon, reverse mortgage proceeds must be handled with absolute care.

Prenuptial Agreements and Medicaid

In second marriages, many assume their assets are protected by a prenuptial agreementThey are not.

Medicaid treats married couples' assets as **joint property**, no matter what the prenup says. If one spouse needs long-term care and they don't have long-term care insurance, the assets of **both spouses** must be spent down.

Medicaid Estate Recovery

Federal law requires states to recover Medicaid long-term care costs from the estates of recipients age 55 or older.

This means the state can recover:

- real estate
- personal property
- assets included in the estate under state probate law
- other property in which the recipient had an interest at death

If a surviving spouse lives in the home, recovery usually waits until that spouse passes away. States often place a Medicaid lien on the home.

There is one major exception: If an adult child lived with the parent for **2+ years**, and their presence prevented nursing home placement, the home may be transferred to that child without penalty.

Transferring Assets: "I'll Just Give It All Away!"

It doesn't work.

Medicaid enforces a **5-year look-back period** on all transfers.

If someone gave away assets for less than fair market value within the last 60 months, the state will impose a penalty period of ineligibility based on the amount transferred.

This applies to both direct transfers and transfers to trusts.

Examples of How Transfers Can Backfire

Divorce

If parents gave $120,000 to their daughter Marcy six years ago, it wouldn't create a Medicaid penalty. As of this writing in 2025.

But if Marcy divorces, the money becomes marital property, she could lose half.

Lawsuits

If Marcy and her husband are sued, the $120,000 in their joint account could be taken in a judgment.

Financial Aid

That $120,000 counts as Marcy and her husband's asset. Their child may lose eligibility for financial aid.

"Buying Toys"

Even well-meaning adult children may be tempted to "borrow" the money. The risk of misuse or loss is high.

Bottom Line

Medicaid rules are complex and constantly changing. Poor planning, and especially improper gifting, can destroy eligibility. Before transferring money, taking a reverse mortgage, or assuming assets are protected, families should talk with a qualified elder law attorney.

Ray Alkalai

Chapter 7:

The Complete Guide to Long Term Care Insurance, Without the Confusion

How Much Does Long-Term Care Insurance Cost?

The price of long-term care insurance depends on the benefits and options you choose. More features mean higher premiums. But one thing is always true: **premiums will never cost as much as even a few months in a nursing home without insurance.**

Even though long-term care insurance is the most cost-effective way to prepare, many people feel the premiums are out of reach. To help solve this problem, the federal government created the **Long-Term Care Partnership Program**.

The Partnership Program protects part of your assets if you use your policy and later need Medicaid. Whatever your policy pays out becomes the amount of assets you're allowed to keep if you apply for Medicaid. These protected assets are also exempt from Medicaid estate recovery.

Traditional Long-Term Care Insurance (use it or lose it policy)

Years ago, these policies were considered "nursing-home insurance." Today, they cover far more:

- in-home care
- adult day care
- assisted living
- nursing-home care

They're now viewed as **keep my lifestyle insurance**, designed to support independence and choice.

Who Cannot Get Long-Term Care Insurance?

Understanding Underwriting

When you apply, the insurance company reviews your medical history. They check for conditions such as Alzheimer's disease, Parkinson's, MS, cognitive impairment, or a major stroke with lasting impact. These conditions typically disqualify applicants.

Cancer survivors often qualify once treatment-free for a certain period. Height and weight are also considered. Some companies request a nurse visit or conduct a brief phone interview.

Every insurer uses its own underwriting guidelines, so it's important to ask questions before applying.

Qualifying to Use Long-Term Care Benefits

Activities of Daily Living (ADLs)

To access a **tax-qualified** long-term care policy, the insured must need help with **2 out of 6 ADLs** for at least **90 days**, certified by a licensed healthcare practitioner. In most cases the 90 day count is counted as days of service. So if you only get help 3 days a week, it take time to count to 90 days.

The 6 ADLs are:

- bathing
- dressing
- eating
- toileting
- continence
- transferring (moving from bed to chair)

Or the insured must have a **cognitive impairment**, such as dementia. These individuals may be physically capable yet unable to remember or logically perform tasks safely.

Comprehensive vs. Facility-Only Plans

Comprehensive Plans

Cover:

- in-home care
- adult day care
- assisted living
- nursing homes

These plans provide flexibility and help people stay at home longer.

Facility-Only Plans

Cover only assisted living and nursing-home care. They are less expensive and may fit people without nearby family support. However, **benefits cannot be used for care received at home**.

Benefit Period

The benefit period is how long the policy will pay for care. Options include: 2, 3, 4, 5, 7, 10 years, or lifetime coverage.

Premiums may be paid for decades, but the policy only lasts as long as the benefit period chosen.

To decide on the right period, review your personal and family health history. Chronic conditions such as Alzheimer's, Parkinson's, MS, or ALS may require longer coverage.

Average care durations:

- Nursing home: **2.8 years**
- In-home caregiving: **4.1 years**

Daily Benefit Amount

This is the maximum amount the policy pays per day, week, or month. Know your local costs. The national average for a semi-private nursing home room in 2024 was **$305 per day** or **$9,150 per month.**

Private rooms cost more and should be factored into planning.

Some families use Social Security or pension income to cover part of care, allowing for a smaller daily benefit. But remember: the daily rate covers only room and board. Medications, incontinence supplies, and other necessities can add **20% more** per day.

Elimination Period

This works like a deductible. It's the waiting period before benefits begin. Common options are: 0, 30, 60, 90, 100, or 180 days.

Shorter periods mean higher premiums.

Some companies count one day of home care as **seven days** toward the elimination period. Others may require actual service days, **which can stretch the waiting period** over many weeks if care is infrequent.

Inflation Protection

Healthcare costs rise **4–7% per year**. Without inflation protection, today's $350/day can reach $500/day or more within a decade.

Options include:

- **5% Compound Inflation:** Best for buyers under 70. Most complete protection.

- **5% Simple Inflation:** Grows steadily but slower than compound. Often recommended for ages 70+.
- **Future Purchase Option:** Lets you buy additional coverage later. Premiums adjust only when you add benefits.

Care Coordination

Some policies include care coordination, a professional nurse or social worker who helps identify the best local services and create a care plan.

This benefit removes guesswork, reduces stress, and ensures quality care. Coordinators are guides, not gatekeepers.

Home and Community Care Benefits

Covers services from licensed providers, including:

- nursing care
- physical, occupational, and speech therapy
- nurse's aides
- homemaker services
- hospice
- adult day care

Some enhanced plans reimburse friends or family who provide care, though most policies will not pay a spouse.

Facility Care

Covers care in nursing homes, assisted-living facilities, and hospice centers. Policies generally pay for room and board, personal care, and nursing support.

Most include a **bed reservation benefit**, holding your room for up to 30 days when you leave temporarily.

Respite Care

Provides relief for family caregivers. Policies typically cover up to **21 days per year** for respite care, and no elimination period is required.

Alternate Plan of Care

Allows coverage for non-traditional services that improve safety or independence, such as:

- emergency alert systems
- wheelchair ramps

The insurer must approve these services.

Caregiver Training

Policies often pay to train an informal caregiver, ensuring safe and effective care at home.

Riders: Extra Features That Add Flexibility

Shared Benefits

Allows spouses to share one combined pool of benefits.

Survivorship

If both spouses have policies with no claims for 7–10 years and one dies, the surviving spouse's policy becomes paid-up.

Return of Premium

Refunds premiums to heirs if no claims were made. Each company designs this differently.

Waiver of Premium

Premiums stop once benefits begin, usually after the elimination period.

Indemnity Plans

Instead of reimbursement, these plans pay the insured directly. They offer more flexibility but cost more.

Important Factors When Choosing a Policy

Company Ratings

Choose companies with **A or better** AM Best ratings as well as companies with a solid track record.

Company Assets

Long Term Care – It Doesn't Have To Be Expensive

Look for insurers with **billions** in assets.

Discounts

Many companies offer:

- spousal or partner discounts (30–50%)
- good health discounts (10–15%)
- group or affinity discounts for certain organizations

Tax Considerations

Premiums for tax-qualified policies count as medical expenses. When total medical expenses exceed **7.5% of adjusted gross income**, part of the premium may be deductible.

Business owners, especially those with C-corporations, can often deduct the full cost. Speak to a tax advisor.

Twenty six states offer deductions or credits for long-term care insurance premiums. Rules vary, so check with a tax advisor.

Tax-Qualified vs. Non-Tax-Qualified Plans

Tax-Qualified Plans

- Follow HIPAA rules
- Require help with **2 of 6 ADLs** for **90+ days**
- Benefits are not taxable
- Policies are guaranteed renewable

Non-Tax-Qualified Plans

- Require help with **1 of 5 ADLs**
- Benefits may be taxable (ongoing debate)
- Generally more expensive

Payment Options

Annual Premium

Paid yearly, quarterly, semi-annually, or monthly (with small fees). Premiums stop once benefits begin.

10-Pay

Higher premiums for 10 years; then paid-up for life.

Pay to 65

Premiums end at age 65, ideal for those retiring.

Lump-Sum

One-time payment with no future premiums. Popular with business owners and used in **asset-based long-term care designs.**

Chapter 8:

Turn Existing Annuities Into Tax Free Long-Term Care Benefits, Even With Health Issues

The Pension Protection Act of 2006

On August 17, 2006, the Pension Protection Act (PPA) became law. This Act changed how annuities can be used by allowing long-term care (LTC) benefits to be attached to annuity contracts, and offering valuable tax advantages along the way.

What the Pension Protection Act Allows

The Act gives consumers two major benefits:

1. Use Annuity Cash Value to Pay LTC Premiums (Tax-Advantaged)

The cash value inside an annuity can be used to pay long term care insurance premiums.
When this happens:

- LTC premiums are paid using existing annuity value
- The annuity's cost basis is reduced
- No taxable event occurs

2. Tax-Free 1035 Exchanges Into LTC-Friendly Annuities

The PPA allows a tax-free 1035 exchange from a traditional annuity into a new annuity with an LTC rider.

This is especially helpful for:

- people with annuities that have large gains and low cost basis
- individuals with health conditions who may not qualify for traditional LTC insurance

This provision became effective for exchanges after 2009.

Post-COVID Developments

Since COVID-19, more insurers now offer **guaranteed-issue PPA-compliant annuities**, making it easier for people with significant health issues, or already receiving care, to get coverage. This can even help those newly diagnosed with one of the **70+ types of dementia**.

How an Annuity-Based LTC Strategy Works

Dave's Story (Age 70)

Dave is recently widowed. His children live out of town, and he has several health challenges:

- insulin-dependent diabetes
- a history of heart disease

Because of these conditions, he didn't qualify for traditional long-term care insurance. However, he did own a **$140,000 fixed annuity** with a **$40,000 cost basis**.

By using a **1035 exchange** to move his annuity into a PPA-compliant LTC annuity, Bob gained significant advantages:

What Dave Had Before

- $140,000 fixed annuity
- Earning interest but offering no LTC leverage

What Dave Gained After

By repositioning the same $140,000 into a PPA-qualified LTC annuity:

- His annuity **continues to earn interest**
- He receives a **$420,000 long-term care benefit pool**

- Benefits can be used for:
    - home care
    - assisted living
    - skilled nursing care
- **No annual premiums**
- As the annuity grows, the LTC pool, potentially, grows too *(assuming benefits are not used)*

Summary

Dave turned $140,000 of existing assets into **three times** the amount available for long-term care, tax-advantaged and without medical underwriting barriers that traditional LTC insurance requires.

Not all products are available in all states. Examples are hypothetical and not guaranteed. Always consult a tax or care funding professional.

Chapter 9:

When Long-Term Care Is Needed Now: A Smart Strategy Many Families Overlook

For many years, using an immediate annuity to pay for long-term care didn't seem practical. That changed as more older adults began needing extended care and insurance companies started creating new options. With the first wave of baby boomers turning 75 in 2021, insurers introduced **individually underwritten immediate annuities**, a strategy built specifically for people already facing health challenges.

How Individually Underwritten Immediate Annuities Work

These annuities are different from traditional ones because the insurance company reviews the applicant's medical records before making an offer. This medical review often allows the insurer to pay **up to three times more income** than a standard immediate annuity would.

These plans are especially helpful for people who already need care and can't perform **two of the six activities of daily living**—eating, dressing, bathing, transferring, toileting, or continence—or who have cognitive impairment. Because benefits start right away, the income can be used immediately to pay for:

- Home health care
- Assisted living
- Skilled nursing care
- Care provided by a chosen caregiver, including family members

This gives families flexibility and allows many seniors to stay where they feel most comfortable.

Example: Jane's Story

Jane is 69, widowed, and living with Parkinson's disease. Her daughter has been caring for her at home but must return to work to earn her $3,000 monthly income. Sue can pay her own living expenses but worries her savings won't last if she also pays her daughter to keep providing care.

Jane has **$200,000 in savings** and **$160,000 in an IRA**, but she wants a solution that helps her stay at home, pay her daughter fairly, and still protect her long-term financial security.

Through an individually underwritten immediate annuity, Jane secures:

- A **$6,917 per month long-term care benefit**
- A **$500,000 tax-free death benefit** for her children if she never needs care
- The ability to choose **where** she receives care and **who** provides it

All of this is funded through a plan with an **annual premium of $1,110**, structured for her specific health situation.

This approach gives Jane the independence she wants and the financial protection her family needs.

Keep in mind, these plans change over time so reach out to a care funding specialist to see what is available and what you qualify for.

Ray Alkalai

Chapter 10:

The Smart Money Move... Protect Your Savings Without 'Use It or Lose It' Insurance

Turning "Just In Case Money" Into Protection

Many retirees have "Just In Case" money set aside for emergencies, not for everyday living. If everything goes well, these dollars eventually pass to children, a church, or a favorite charity. But one threat can wipe out those assets fast: the rising cost of long-term care.

Because of this risk, many people try to "self-insure," meaning they plan to pay out of pocket if care is ever needed. The problem is that long-term care can cost $60,000–$100,000 per year or more. A few years of care can drain even strong portfolios.

Asset based long term care strategies offer a smarter middle ground. Instead of buying traditional LTC insurance with ongoing premiums, you reposition a portion of your legacy assets into a specially designed life insurance policy or annuity that multiplies your funds if care is needed, and passes money to your heirs if it's not. **(this is what happened with my mothers policy)**

How the Strategy Works

Money is moved from its current account, like a savings account, CD, or fixed annuity that is not being used, into a life insurance policy or an annuity with LTC benefits. These riders allow the benefit to be used during life to pay for long-term care in the home, assisted living, or a nursing facility.

Depending on age, health, and benefit design, every dollar placed into the policy can be worth **two to five times more** for long-term care. If care is never needed, the remaining value passes to heirs usually income-tax-free. And in most policies, there is a money-back guarantee that allows the owner to reclaim their premium if the plan no longer fits their needs.

This isn't about "buying insurance." It's about **moving money from one pocket to the other,** into a safer, more efficient place that protects against one of retirement's biggest risks.

Why Multiplying the Benefit Matters

Because long-term care is so expensive and the average need lasts more than two years, most asset-based plans include an extension rider. This rider expands the total available benefit, often doubling or tripling what the client originally deposited.

For example, depositing **$50,000** can create **$250,000** in total long-term care benefits and provide up to six years of protection. This example is a general idea of what the math will look like. Speak to a specialist for what you qualify for.

For People Who Dislike Traditional LTC Insurance

This approach is ideal for:

- People who don't want to pay annual premiums
- People who don't like the "use it or lose it" nature of traditional LTC policies
- People who plan to use their own assets for care
- People who want to keep control, choose where they receive care, and pass unused money to heirs

Asset-based strategies solve all these concerns and still protect the portfolio from being drained by care costs.

An Alternative for Those Who Prefer Annuities

Some people simply don't want life insurance of any kind. For them, insurance companies offer another option: **fixed index annuities with guaranteed income riders.** These riders **double the income** if the owner enters a nursing home.

This gives retirees the ability to turn part of their assets into dependable income that increases when care is needed.

Why This Strategy Matters

Long-term care is one of the hardest and most expensive risks in retirement financially and emotionally. Asset-based long-term care strategies give consumers a way to stay in control, protect their savings, avoid large annual premiums, and still leave a meaningful legacy if care is never needed.

Since the money must be invested somewhere anyway, these plans offer a safe and flexible place to store it, while multiplying its power if life takes an unexpected turn.

Chapter 11:

A Smarter Way to Use Your IRA: Care Benefits and Legacy in One Move

Using IRA Dollars for Long-Term Care

Many retirees rely on their IRA for income later in life. Others wait until age 73 and some will till 75, when required minimum distributions (RMDs) begin. But there's another option: using a portion of an IRA to fund a long-term care strategy.

This approach uses an **IRA-based annuity** that pays out internally over 10 years to fund a life insurance policy with long-term care benefits. The annuity itself is the IRA. Each year for 10 years, part of the annuity is automatically moved into the life insurance policy. That amount shows up on a **1099-R** as a taxable IRA distribution.

For people who have more "qualified" money (IRA dollars) than after-tax savings, this can be a powerful way to turn tax-deferred funds into long-term care protection.

Example: Jeff, Age 60

Jeff is recently widowed, retired, and financially stable. His biggest concern is how to pay for long-term care someday. Like many people, most of his money is in his IRA, not in after-tax accounts.

Jeff uses a **tax-free trustee-to-trustee transfer** to move **$157,000** from his $500,000 IRA into an IRA-based annuity. This annuity then funds a 10-pay life insurance policy that provides:

- **$237,000 death benefit** for his children
- **$9,488 per month** in long-term care benefits
- Coverage for home care, assisted living, adult day care, or skilled nursing care

Jeff still keeps the remaining **$343,000** in his IRA.

Example: A Married Couple Using the Same Strategy

Sue (60) and Jim (65) worry about long-term care but dislike traditional long-term care insurance because of ongoing premiums. They also want to help their children avoid the tax bill that comes when both parents have passed away and the IRA becomes fully taxable.

Jim decides to transfer **$240,000** from his IRA into an IRA annuity. This annuity funds a **second-to-die life insurance policy** covering both spouses. Each year, Jim receives a 1099-R for the amount the annuity transfers into the policy.

Their results:

- **$290,000 tax-free death benefit** for their children
- **$9,049 per month** in long-term care benefits, available for both Sue and Jim for life
- Coverage for home health, assisted living, adult day care, or skilled nursing care

This gives the couple meaningful long-term care protection without ongoing premium payments and reduces the future tax burden on their heirs.

Why This Strategy Works

For retirees who have substantial IRA assets and want long-term care protection without traditional insurance premiums, this approach provides:

- Predictable 10-year funding, benefits usually start day one of policy
- Large tax-free death benefits
- Lifetime long-term care benefits
- A way to reposition IRA dollars efficiently
- Better control over where and how care is received

It turns taxable IRA money into a long-term care safety net, while still protecting family inheritance.

Ray Alkalai

Chapter 12:

The Legal Documents Every Family Must Have Before Care Is Needed

Get the Legal Paperwork in Place

One of the most important parts of long-term care planning is making sure your legal documents are complete and up to date. A **durable power of attorney for health care**, a **financial power of attorney**, and an **advanced directive or living will** are essential.

An elder law attorney can help you prepare:

- Trusts
- Wills
- Durable powers of attorney
- Medicaid and VA benefit planning
- Advanced medical directives
- Other important legal documents

It is very important that you have all your documents and beneficiary designations in place as it makes taking care of you and your care provider's life much easier. Trying to get things done efficiently when you are already incapacitated is very difficult and costly.

Understanding the Power of Attorney (POA)

A **power of attorney (POA)** allows one person (the *principal*) to authorize another person (the *agent*) to act on their behalf. POAs are commonly used for **financial decisions** and **health care decisions**, and most states treat these as two separate legal tools. Because of this, it's best to create **two POAs**, one for finances, one for medical decisions.

When to Have a Financial POA

A financial POA helps people with physical limitations manage day-to-day tasks like banking. It also serves an important protective role. If you lose mental capacity and do **not** have a durable POA, your family may need to go to court to get a guardian or conservator appointed, an expensive and time consuming process.

A **durable POA** continues to work even if you become mentally incapacitated. Without the "durable" wording, the POA becomes invalid the moment you lose capacity.

Warning: some banks do not make it easy for the POA. Be ready for a challenge.

What Makes a POA "Durable"?

Durability is defined by state law. Under the Uniform Durable Power of Attorney Act (used in 48 states), a POA is durable only if the written document includes language such as:

- "This power of attorney shall not be affected by subsequent disability or incapacity of the principal," or
- "This power of attorney shall become effective upon the disability or incapacity of the principal."

The POA must be written and signed, and most states require it to be **notarized**, especially for real estate transactions. Some states also require witnesses.

Advanced Directives (Living Wills)

An **advanced directive** may be the most important document you'll ever create. It tells your loved ones and health care providers exactly what you want at the end of life if you can't speak for yourself.

Common advanced directives include:

- **Living wills**—instructing doctors on life support decisions when someone is permanently unconscious or terminally ill
- **Durable powers of attorney for health care**—appointing someone to make medical decisions if you become incapacitated

When properly drafted, these documents protect family members and medical providers who follow your wishes. Elder law attorneys can help you complete them, and many hospitals offer forms and notary services at admission.

"Five Wishes"

One well-known advanced directive is **Five Wishes**, which covers medical, personal, emotional, and spiritual preferences. It helps you communicate:

- Who should make health care decisions for you
- What treatments you want or do not want
- Your comfort preferences
- How you want others to treat you
- What you want loved ones to know

More information is available at www.agingwithdignity.org.

Revocable Living Trusts

A **revocable living trust** is created by an individual (the trustor) and managed by a trustee. The trustor can serve as their own trustee while they are alive and mentally able. When the trustor dies, a successor trustee takes over.

A living trust:

- Avoids probate
- Speeds up distribution of assets
- Offers privacy because probate is public
- Is harder to contest than a will

The drawbacks: sometimes cost, setting one up takes more time, requires ongoing updates, and assets must be retitled into the trust.

Irrevocable Trusts

An **irrevocable trust** transfers ownership and control away from the grantor permanently. The trust becomes a separate taxable entity and pays tax on income it retains. Because the grantor gives up control, irrevocable trusts are used mainly for advanced estate planning strategies.

A home placed in an irrevocable trust is **usually not eligible** for a reverse mortgage.

Transfer on Death Deed

In some states, as in Minnesota, you can transfer a property on death which helps avoid probate. The process is pretty simple and if you have no issues with who gets what then this may be a very cost effective way to transfer a property when you pass.

Ray Alkalai

Chapter 13:

Medicaid Myths vs. Reality: How Smart Planning Protects Your Life Savings

When Medicaid Becomes the Only Path

Medicaid should always be a last resort for long-term care, but sometimes it's the only realistic way to protect a family's remaining assets. This usually happens in two situations:

1. When one spouse needs nursing home care
2. When a single person is at risk of losing everything to care costs

Understanding the rules can help families avoid unnecessary financial loss.

Medicaid Planning for Married Couples

How Asset Division Works

Federal law allows a couple to split their countable assets when one spouse enters a nursing home. The healthy spouse, known as the **community spouse**, may keep *half* of the assets up to **$157,920** (2025 limit in MN).

Example:
Keri (78) and Scott (82) live in Minnesota with **$480,000** in countable assets.

- Split in half: $240,000 each
- But the community spouse limit is $157,920
- That means **$322,080** must be "spent down" to about **$11,000** before Medicaid steps in

Most families assume there's no way around this. But there is a potential way.

Using OBRA '93 to Protect the Assets

The **Omnibus Reconciliation Act of 1993 (OBRA '93)** allows the community spouse to protect those "excess" assets by turning them into income using a **Medicaid-compliant annuity**.

To qualify, the annuity must be:

- Irrevocable
- Non-assignable
- Non-commutable
- Non-transferable
- Actuarially sound (this is where an attorney has to be involved)

When structured correctly, the community spouse can legally keep **100%** of the assets, and the spouse entering care qualifies for Medicaid immediately.

As a warning, this must be done in coordination with an elder law attorney to avoid making a mistake. NOT ALL elder law attorneys are well versed in Medicaid Compliant Annuity's.

Medicaid Planning for Single Individuals

Protecting assets is harder for a single person, but still possible.

Current Medicaid rules often allow a person to protect **25–50%** of their assets by combining:

- A transfer to children or an irrevocable trust
- A Medicaid compliant annuity to privately pay during the penalty period

Example: Marge

Marge (80) enters a nursing home with $150,000 in an IRA and $150,000 in cash—too much to qualify for Medicaid.

A planning strategy could look like this:

1. Transfer **$150,000** to an irrevocable trust
2. Move the remaining **$150,000 IRA** into a Medicaid compliant annuity
3. Use the annuity income, plus Social Security and pension, to pay for care during the **31-month** penalty created by the transfer

After the penalty ends, Marge becomes Medicaid eligible and has **$150,000** protected for final needs or her children.

Again, an attorney or a well versed Medicaid compliant annuity specialists must be used to avoid government issues.

Chapter 14:

Aid & Attendance: The Tax Free Income Most Veterans Never Hear About

The Aid & Attendance Benefit: A Hidden Lifeline

The Veterans Administration offers a little-known pension called **Aid and Attendance (A&A)**. It provides extra tax-free income to veterans or surviving spouses who need help with everyday tasks like bathing, dressing, eating, or managing continence. It also helps those who are blind, have cognitive decline, or live in a nursing home.

This benefit is not for simple housekeeping or occasional help. But it *does* cover care at home, in assisted living, or in a nursing home. Many families overlook it, even when it could make the difference between safe care and financial strain.

This is a **pension benefit**, not a disability benefit. It does **not** require a service-related injury. Many veterans who qualify never hear about it unless a professional guides them.

Who Can Qualify?

To be eligible, a veteran must have served **90 days of active duty**, including **one day during a wartime period** (does not need to be in combat zone). The VA defines wartime service as:

- **WWI:** 4/16/1917 – 11/11/1918
- **WWII:** 12/7/1941 – 12/31/1946
- **Korea:** 6/25/1950 – 1/31/1955
- **Vietnam:** 8/5/1964 – 5/7/1975
- **Persian Gulf:** 8/2/1990 – present

Many veterans meet these rules and qualify medically but never apply because they were told incorrectly that they "have too much money."

Two Veterans, One Benefit

Consider two veterans who served side-by-side in WWII and now live in the same assisted living facility.

Veteran #1

He lived a fast life—multiple divorces, gambling, little savings—only **$35,000** left. Within a year he ran out of money. When he couldn't pay the facility, he was discharged. No family helped. His new girlfriend disappeared.

He moved to a Medicaid nursing home **50 miles away**. He lost most of his **$1,800+ VA pension**, reduced to **$90 per month** because Medicaid rules don't allow "double dipping." He was miserable, isolated, and angry.

Veteran #2

He was steady—married for 40+ years, raised three daughters, saved **$438,000**. With his resources and the Aid & Attendance pension, he stayed in assisted living for **4½ years** and never needed a nursing home. He received over **$117,000 in tax-free VA income**.

Who Deserves the Pension?

Both did.

Both served in wartime. Lifestyle shouldn't decide who qualifies. But the reality is that **middle-class wartime veterans benefit the most** because they have enough assets to stay in assisted living but need extra income to close the gap.

Poor veterans often end up on Medicaid with the pension reduced to $90. Wealthy veterans rarely need the help. But those with **$250,000–$750,000** in assets, our typical middle class vets, gain the most stability and independence.

Clearing Up the Biggest Misunderstanding

Most people think you must be poor to qualify. That's wrong.

As of **2025**, a veteran or surviving spouse can have up to **$163,699** in total assets and still qualify, as long as they also meet medical and income rules.

With proper planning, many become eligible the **first day of the next month** after applying. However, approval may take **6-8 months**, so retroactive benefits are paid back to the first eligible month.

How Much Does A&A Pay?

In **2025**, maximum monthly A&A benefits are:

- **Veteran:** $2,358
- **Surviving spouse:** $1,515
- **Married veteran needing care:** $2,795

All tax-free. (see a tax advisor)

For many families, this extra income covers the gap between Social Security and the cost of assisted living or home care.

What If Assets Exceed the Limit?

Veterans with extra assets can reposition money into certain approved investments. Three rules should guide the planning:

1. **Safety of principal**
2. **Adequate liquidity**
3. **Better earning potential than a bank CD**

These moves must be done carefully because Aid & Attendance has a **3-year look-back period**. Planning at 73 makes eligibility possible at 76. Waiting until age 91 pushes eligibility to 94. **Delays cost families real money and care options.**

Planning must be supervised by a **VA-accredited attorney** or a qualified professional. Done incorrectly, it can destroy future Medicaid eligibility.

Why This Matters

Veterans earned this pension through wartime service. The benefit exists so they don't live in unsafe, low-quality environments in old age. Most use it to pay for **home care** or an **assisted-living apartment**, helping them avoid a nursing home.

It takes planning and patience, but the payoff can be life-changing.

Two Key Questions

1. **Do you have a child you trust completely?**
2. **Can you imagine either spouse needing extended care in the next 25 years?**

If the answer is yes, it's time to explore the benefit.

Applying is free. Getting guidance is smart. And for many families, Aid & Attendance is the missing piece that keeps a veteran safe, stable, and at home.

Ray Alkalai

Chapter 15:

Don't Go It Alone: How to Pick Advisors Who Actually Know Long-Term Care

When you're facing a long-term care crisis with an aging parent, you need a clear plan, not guesswork. A solid Eldercare financial plan becomes your roadmap for paying for home care, assisted living, or nursing home expenses in the most tax-smart, cost-efficient way possible. A skilled professional should also review Medicaid and Veterans benefits to help reduce out-of-pocket costs.

What to Expect From a Qualified Professional

A capable long-term care advisor should provide:

1. **Clear understanding of care needs and costs.**
2. **A full review of income, expenses, cash flow, taxes, assets, and health risks.**
3. **A written plan explained in simple, understandable language.**

4. **Implementation and coordination** with elder law attorneys for Medicaid or VA applications when needed, plus regular reviews and updates.

Choose someone with real long-term care planning experience and connections to a senior care community that can help make the process smoother. It makes all the difference.

Understanding Investment Advisors

What Is a Financial Professional?

An financial professional is a person or firm paid to give advice about securities such as stocks, bonds, mutual funds, or exchange-traded funds. Some also manage investment portfolios.

How Is an Financial Professional Different From a Financial Planner/Advisor?

Many financial professionals are investment advisors /planners, but not all investment advisors/planners are Care Funding Specialists. Some look at your entire financial life, insurance, savings, taxes, estate planning, and retirement. Others only recommend a limited set of products.

Before hiring anyone, make sure you understand:

- Exactly what services they provide
- Any limits on what they can recommend
- How they're paid
- What you're paying for

Smart Questions to Ask

Before you hire a professional of any kind, ask:

- What experience do you have with people in my situation?
- What is your education and employment history?
- What licenses do you hold?
- Are you registered with the SEC, a state, or FINRA?
- What products and services do you offer?
- Are you limited to certain products?
- How are you paid—hourly, flat fee, commissions, or a percentage of assets?
- Have you ever been disciplined or sued by a client?
- Will you send me both parts of your Form ADV?

Always meet the professional in person to see if you feel comfortable with them. Yes virtual counts in todays world.

Keep in mind, every industry has great and horrible professionals. You can have all the licensing and designations in the world and still be a bad idea. Character is hard to judge, so use your inner voice. If it sounds questionable, ask questions! Don't be shy.

How Investment Advisors Get Paid

Investment advisors are generally paid in one or more of the following ways:

- A percentage of the assets they manage
- An hourly fee
- A flat fee
- Commissions
- A combination of the above

Each method has pros and cons. Ask the professional to explain them clearly, and ask if their fee is negotiable. Make sure to ask them what the long term fee looks like as well.

Elder Law Attorneys

Aging adults and their families deal with legal issues that can quickly get complicated. Elder law attorneys understand the laws that impact seniors and can help avoid costly mistakes.

They can assist with:

- Trusts
- Wills
- Durable powers of attorney
- Medicaid and VA benefits
- Advanced medical directives
- Other related documents

The National Academy of Elder Law Attorneys (NAELA) at **www.naela.org** is the leading organization in this field. Look for an attorney who regularly handles nursing home and Medicaid cases—not someone who only sees a few per year.

Care Consultant: A Hidden Gem

A care consultant can be one of your best resources when you're trying to coordinate care. These professionals understand local services, family dynamics, medical needs, and long term care options.

They help with:

- Assessments
- Creating a care plan
- Arranging services
- Monitoring quality of care
- Coordinating transitions to new living arrangements

Care consultants are often former nurses, social workers, therapists, or gerontologists. They can also help with bill paying, housekeeping, transportation, meal delivery, and personal care.

They act as advocates—especially valuable when family lives far away. Long term care insurance may cover some or all of their fees.

To find a care manager, visit **www.aginglifecare.org**.

Tips for Choosing a Care Manager

- Ask for references and company information
- Check the Better Business Bureau

- Understand fees, contracts, and extra charges (some work for free for you)
- Ask about their availability
- Clarify how often they communicate and by what method (phone, email, etc.)

When a Parent Refuses Help

Most aging parents don't want to admit they need help. They may deny problems like missed bills, falls, confusion, or poor hygiene. Many don't want their children involved in personal or financial matters.

How to Start the Conversation

There is no perfect approach, but these tips can help:

- Choose a quiet, private time, not a holiday or family gathering.
- Avoid blaming. Focus on how *you* feel: "I'm worried about you, and here's why."
- Ask a geriatric care manager for guidance, they've had this conversation hundreds of times.
- Explain that meeting with a professional will give *both* of you peace of mind.
- Remind them that a neutral third party may feel less threatening than advice coming from their children.
- If safety is a concern, the care manager can explain that decisions need to be made now, before someone else makes them later.

A respectful, calm approach usually works best.

Ray Alkalai

Chapter 16:

Why "I'll Self-Insure" Is the Most Expensive Myth in Long-Term Care

"I'll Self-Insure"

Every long-term care plan is a form of self-insurance. The real question is whether you want to shoulder all the risk alone or use strategies that create more leverage, tax advantages, and protection for your family.

Insurance companies aren't handing out free benefits. You still use your own money, but in return, they put up theirs too. That leverage can multiply your dollars for care.

A Simple Example

If you've earmarked **$300,000** in your portfolio for care, you could reposition **$100,000** into a plan that offers **3:1 leverage**, while the remaining **$200,000** stays invested. That gives your financial advisor *more* assets to manage, plus you gain long-term care benefits. Everyone wins.

And if you ever need care, you'll probably spend that same $300,000 anyway. Why not use **$200,000 of the insurance company's money, income-tax-free**, instead of draining your own? Especially if you do it right and don't use it, you pass it to family.

"But My Advisor Told Me I Can Self-Insure…"

If we had a nickel for every time someone heard this…

Most advisors mean well, but few would tell you to self-insure your health insurance or skip homeowners insurance because "you'll be fine." Yet long-term care is far more likely to happen and far more expensive.

Ask your advisor to put in writing that you should self-insure your long-term care risk. You already know how that email goes.

Here's the truth: Most advisors don't specialize in long-term care. They may not know the current options, be contracted to offer them, or want to deal with the complexity. That doesn't make them bad, just not equipped for this area.

Test Your Portfolio

Run a portfolio projection to age 80. Now add in:

- a **20% market drop**,
- an additional **$20,000 per month** in care costs for you and your spouse,
- and your usual withdrawals.

See how long your assets last.

Your advisor won't be the one writing the nursing home check. You will. So ask them directly:
"If my assets can't cover care, will you pay the difference?"

The answer matters.

"It's Too Expensive"

People say this long before they've even seen numbers. If someone claims it's too costly, ask them, **"How much is it?"** The room usually goes quiet.

Instead, compare the cost of coverage to:

- years of full-time care,
- the emotional strain on your family,
- and the financial hit to your spouse or heirs.

Long-term care is only "expensive" until you see the value. Then it becomes clear what's actually costly—paying for care without any leverage at all.

"I'm Not Healthy Enough to Qualify"

This is another common fear, but it may not be true.

As of **2023**, there are **guaranteed-issue** long-term care plans that accept people regardless of health. These specific options may not last forever, but there are also strategies using standard fixed or indexed annuities that can still create leverage for care, protect assets, and support retirement income.

Most people never hear about these tools because they aren't widely taught or discussed. Long-term care planning is a specialized corner of the financial world, and most professionals simply don't work in it.

Here's the reality: If someone who is already in care could go back in time to put leverage in place, nearly all of them would. Their families would too.

At least explore your options. If you decide it isn't right for you, no problem, you made an informed choice. But discovering later that you *would* have qualified and waited too long to act... that's a tough family conversation.

Don't let anyone tell you "everything will be fine" without offering an actual guarantee. You get to decide your future, not a financial influencer who won't be there to pay the bills.

Conclusion

Families today look very different than they did a generation ago. Many seniors worry about outliving their money and how they would handle the high cost of long-term care. At the same time, most adult children are pulled in every direction, two-income households, busy schedules, and the quiet fear of what will happen when Mom or Dad can no longer manage on their own.

Most older adults still live at home, often with some level of support. Only **35%** of seniors who need care are in nursing homes, while **65%** receive care in a home-like setting. Staying home matters deeply. Seniors consistently say their biggest fears revolve around losing independence, dignity, and control, not just their health. And nothing fuels those fears more than the idea of running out of money or being forced into a nursing home.

While home care is generally less expensive than nursing-home care, **24/7 in-home care can cost even more than a nursing home**, especially when medical support is needed. Long-term care insurance can help extend the time a senior can safely remain at home, but not everyone can qualify or afford it. Some wait too long; others face health challenges that make traditional insurance impossible.

The good news is that there are still options. Families can take steps to protect dignity, safety, and financial stability, even when long-term care insurance isn't available. Seniors can stay at home longer, and families can feel more confident about the future when they understand the tools and strategies available to them.

The key is simple: **talk early, plan early, and learn what's possible before a crisis hits.** When families educate themselves and communicate openly, they give their loved ones the best chance to stay independent, protected, and supported for as long as possible.

Resources

Go To www.ResourceRay.com for a FREE downloadable pdf of all kinds of senior resources.

Ray Alkalai

Bonus Chapter: long-term care funding checklist & next steps

Quick Guide to Know Your Options, Your Gaps, and Your Next Steps

Step 1: Family Readiness Questionnaire

Score each item 0–2. Add your total at the end.

0 = No
1 = Not sure / partly true
2 = Yes

Health & Risk Awareness
☐ I know my family's history with chronic illness or cognitive decline.
☐ I understand the odds: 70% of people over 65 will need care.
☐ I have a general idea of how much care costs in my state.

Financial Preparedness
☐ I know how much of my income would be available to pay for care.
☐ I know how long my savings would last if I paid out of pocket.
☐ I've run the numbers on a market downturn + care event at the same time.

Asset Positioning
☐ I have assets that could be repositioned (IRA, savings, CDs, non-qualified money).
☐ I understand the tax impact of using my IRA or savings to pay for care.
☐ I have talked with a professional about using leverage instead of self-pay.

Legal Readiness
☐ I have a durable power of attorney (financial & healthcare).
☐ I have an updated will or trust.
☐ My family knows my wishes for care.

Care Preferences
☐ I know where I want care (home, assisted living, memory care).
☐ My family knows who I want involved in my care decisions.
☐ I know whether I want to hire family, outside caregivers, or both.

TOTAL SCORE (out of 30): _____

Step 2: What Your Score Means

0–10: High Risk / No Plan

You're wide open to both financial and emotional crisis. Start planning immediately.
Focus on: guaranteed-issue options, asset repositioning strategies, legal documents, and crisis-planning paths (Medicaid or VA where applicable).

11–20: Partial Plan / Significant Gaps

You have some awareness but are still vulnerable.
Focus on: hybrid LTC coverage, IRA-to-LTC strategies, and comparing self-pay vs. leveraged options.

21–26: Strong Start / Needs Optimization

You've done meaningful prep, but not enough to protect income or assets fully.
Focus on: maximizing leverage, filling funding gaps, and tightening legal docs.

27–30: Well-Positioned / Fine-Tune Only

You're ahead of 90% of families.
Focus on: reviewing coverage amounts, confirming tax efficiency, and updating your plan every 1–2 years.

Step 3: Long-Term Care Funding Checklist

Use this list to confirm you're fully covered and not missing opportunities.

A. Identify Your Funding Strategy

☐ I have compared self-insuring vs. using leverage (2x–10x more funds).
☐ I understand how asset-based LTC works and whether I qualify.
☐ I know if a life insurance policy with an LTC rider makes sense for me.
☐ I've reviewed IRA-based LTC strategies (10-pay, annuity-funded, tax-efficient repositioning).
☐ I know if I qualify for VA Aid & Attendance.
☐ I know if Medicaid planning is relevant for my situation.

B. Protect Income and Assets While You Can

☐ I've reviewed how a long-term care event affects my retirement income plan.
☐ I've considered what happens if care starts during a market downturn.
☐ I've explored options that keep me **at home longer**, not just in a facility.
☐ I've reviewed solutions that allow **family caregivers to be paid**, if desired.

C. Understand Crisis-Planning Options (If You're Already in Decline)

☐ I know about OBRA '93 Medicaid-compliant annuities.
☐ I know how irrevocable trusts or asset protection strategies work.
☐ I know how to preserve a portion of assets even if care is already needed.
☐ I understand the timelines: Medicaid (5-year lookback), VA (3-year rule).

D. Confirm You're Working With the Right Professional

☐ I've spoken with someone experienced specifically in **LTC funding strategies**.
☐ They can explain **hybrid LTC, asset-based plans, IRA-to-LTC, Medicaid,** and **VA**.
☐ They've given me written options—NOT just "self-insure."
☐ They coordinate with elder law attorneys when needed.
☐ They help me compare solutions, not push a single product.

Step 4: Your Next Three Moves

Check the ones that apply to your plan.

☐ Run a self-pay vs. leverage comparison.
☐ Get a quote for hybrid LTC or asset-based plans.
☐ Review IRA repositioning options.
☐ Meet with an elder law attorney to update documents.
☐ Request a VA benefits screening (if eligible).
☐ Evaluate Medicaid planning strategies (if health is declining).
☐ Hold a family meeting to share care preferences.

About the Author

Ray Alkalai has been an insurance and financial professional since 2006 and now serves as a Care Funding Specialist and speaker. Through his work with families, Ray helps translate complex insurance and income strategies into clarity and peace of mind. He regularly speaks at senior-care communities in the Twin Cities, showing worried families how to move from anxiety to actionable plans. Ray's philosophy is simple: it's not just about the product, it's about the strategy behind it. The right strategy builds legacy while protecting what matters most.

You can reach

Ray Alkalai

@ www.CareFundingRay.com

Summary

Ray Alkalai

Long-term care shouldn't wipe out your savings or force your family into crisis decisions. Most people don't realize they have options, until it's too late. This book changes that.

Whether you're planning early or facing care needs right now, you'll learn how to:

- **Pay for care without draining your assets**
- **Use insurance, annuities, IRAs, and home equity wisely**
- **Qualify for Medicaid or VA benefits the right way**
- **Protect your independence and stay at home longer**
- **Shield your family from financial and emotional strain**

The biggest myth is that long-term care means "spend everything, and then hope Medicaid helps." It doesn't have to be that way.

Inside is a clear, practical roadmap that helps you keep control, reduce taxes, and preserve the legacy you've spent a lifetime building.

If you want options instead of fear, and a plan instead of panic, start here.

Ray Alkalai

Long Term Care – It Doesn't Have To Be Expensive

Ray Alkalai

Long Term Care – It Doesn't Have To Be Expensive

Made in the USA
Coppell, TX
13 January 2026

68268572R00075